JohnInnes

Fulgens.

Marbled

Large
Single white

Double blush.

Dwarf
Single white.

Dunwichienses

Falkland

Dundee

Lilac

from Balbithan

Scots Roses

of hedgerows and wild gardens

MARY MCMURTRIE

GARDEN • ART • PRESS

First published 1998
©1998 Mary McMurtrie
World copyright reserved

ISBN 1 870673 26 3

British Library Cataloguing-in-Publication Data
A catalogue record for this book is available from the British Library

Frontispiece: a typical wild Scots Rose

Printed in England on Consort Royal Era Satin paper from the
Donside Paper Company, Aberdeen, by
Garden Art Press, Woodbridge, Suffolk IP12 1DS

To Elspeth and Douglas

The rose of all the world is not for me
I want for my part
Only the little white rose of Scotland
That smells sharp and sweet – and breaks the heart.

Hugh MacDiarmid

Acknowledgements

I have had so much kindness and help in preparing this book that I feel I cannot express my gratitude and thanks adequately. I specially want to thank Dr. Waister for his unfailing help and encouragement and his kindness in giving me the freedom of Kinnaird Village Garden, and for roses, both flowers and cuttings, whenever I required them. My thanks also to Miss Kay Anderson and to Dr. Cusick for advice and for roses to paint, to Mrs. Irene Mackie, formerly of Bent, Laurencekirk, for plants and flowers, and to the many friends who found specimen roses and sent or brought them to me: David Bromley, Douglas and Kathleen Willis, Mrs. Cocker, Bob Rutherford, Mrs. McCance, Mrs. Edel Purvis, Mrs. Iris Strachan, Mrs. P. Taylor, Mrs. S. Reid and Mrs. S. Simpson.

I am most grateful to Mrs. Christine Brogden, Mrs. Anna Buxton and Timothy Clark for their encouragement and help, to Dr. Gordon Smith who took me out so often to search for wild and garden Scots Roses and gave me much helpful advice, to Dr. Peter McEwan, and to my old friend the late Alex Duguid for his tale of Prince Charlie's rose and for plants.

The Royal Horticultural Society, the John Innes Institute and Peter Beales all kindly supplied me with early lists. Library books were brought to me by Mrs. Deirdre Bailey and my grand-daughter Elspeth Haston. Graham Stuart Thomas, Dr. Gordon Rowley, Dr. Peter Waister and Wordsworth Editions Ltd., have all kindly allowed me to use quotations from their works. I have also been able to quote from Gertrude Jekyll and Edward Mawley's *Roses for English Gardens*, from *My Garden in Summer* by E.A. Bowles, and from *The Collected Poems* of Hugh MacDiarmid (Carcanet Press Ltd.).

But above all I am indebted to my daughter Elspeth, who has collected, propagated and grown our collection of Scots Roses over many years, and her husband Douglas, both of whom have helped me in countless ways. It is absolutely true to say, as authors do so often, that without their help this book would never have materialised.

Contents

Preface

$\mathcal{I}$ suppose there have never been so many books of splendid botanical flower paintings as there are at the present day. But this is not another of these; it is much simpler, and takes you, as it were, into a garden of the little Scots Roses, where you can get an impression of their delicate beauty and their surprising variety. If this book gives you pleasure and encourages you to plant some Scots Roses in your own garden for further enjoyment, then it will have achieved its purpose.

This collection of watercolour paintings of the Burnet or Scots Rose is only representative. It could never be complete, for new variations are still appearing among the seedlings, while there are several older named varieties that I have not been able to find, such as 'Staffa', described as blush fading to cream and splashed with pink; 'Painted Lady', which, with petals deep purple above and silvery white below, seems to be very like 'Mary Queen of Scots'; and 'Loch Leven' which no longer grows beside the island castle where Queen Mary was imprisoned (where I went in search of it), and is described as a creamy-blush semi-double rose, heavily mottled and delicately pencilled with rose-pink. I hope these may still be found somewhere, and that others, equally desirable, may turn up to delight us in our gardens.

There is the vexed question of naming the rose. At one time a distinction was made between *R. spinosissima* and *R. pimpinellifolia*, but now they are regarded as one species, to be called *pimpinellifolia* (see Bean Vol. IV, p. 126). The name Burnet Rose was first given by Gerard in 1597, and indeed is still used. Later the name Scots Rose appeared. The word Scotch was first used in connection with the rose in 1775 but, as Dr. Waister says, it now refers so much to whisky and terrier dogs that I agree with him in preferring to use the earlier Scots. After all we call our native pine (*Pinus silvestris*) the Scots Pine.

Mary McMurtrie

Foreword

Never has there been such an interest in plants and gardens. This consuming passion includes, for many people, the history of our garden favourites and their representation by artists in a form far less fleeting than any flower.

The magic eye of the camera can fix a rose on celluloid more or less for ever. What it cannot do is to turn a petal so that we can appreciate the colour and texture on both sides. It cannot incline a flower so that we can see the beauty of the stamens. It does not pay attention to the subtle differences in prickles and hairs, in the toothed edges of the leaves or the difference between leaves on old and new shoots.

In this book of Scots Roses by Mary McMurtrie a different kind of eye has transformed the magic on to paper. An understanding of the important differences between varieties comes from growing many kinds and knowing each as it develops to flowering and matures into characteristic hips. The trained scientific eye can learn to detect and appreciate variations on a theme, but it is the artistic eye only which can revitalise and enhance the subject which it is painting.

This book of evocative paintings of Scots Roses is a valuable record of some of the myriad of different kinds which have survived from their heyday in earlier times. It is also a lesson that, with diligent searching, a significant part of our garden heritage of roses is still around us waiting for the assiduous collector.

The casual observer may experience some difficulty in distinguishing some varieties from others, but it has not been the artist's intention that this book should be a definitive identification manual. What it will surely do is to encourage the reader to look with new eyes at the simple form, the beauty of the colourings, the delicate veining and shading of the petals and last but not least the ferocity of the armature.

I feel that these paintings will make you want to search out some Scots Roses if you do not already know them, and if you do, to appreciate them in much more detail. You too may want to begin growing a part of our Scottish garden heritage.

Dr. Gordon Smith

Scots Roses.
M.McM. 1985.

Double blush Scots Rose from Balbithan

The Scots or Burnet Rose

On the sandy dunes and links, the rocky outcrops and windswept beaches of our long and variable coastline, on river banks and even on the thin stony soil of some of our hill-sides, this little rose spreads its low tangle of prickly bushes, with their tiny leaves and delicate white scented flowers. It is characterised by its extremely prickly stems, its five-petalled, solitary white flowers on short leafy sprigs set alternately along the branches, its tiny leaflets, usually rounded and finely notched, its fresh, delicious scent, and in autumn its round dark hips, from deep maroon to black. It is the hardiest of roses, standing full exposure to sun, wind and salt spray, and thriving on the poorest of soils. It is not confined to Scotland, but is widespread, ranging from Iceland east to Siberia, Turkey and Central Asia; it is common throughout Europe to as far south as Armeria in Spain. I have been told of a little Burnet Rose found growing on the Sierra de Albarracin, north-west of Teruel, high on the sub-alpine meadows where the 'Angel's Tears' narcissus flowers in spring, and of a hedge of Burnet Roses in a Russian garden, and again of how it flowers in Ireland among the wind-swept, shattered-limestone pavements of the Burren.

Naming the Rose

Originally the Scots Rose was called the 'Pimpinell Rose' or *Rosa pimpinellifolia* or *R. spinosissima*. It is also known as the Burnet Rose. The name *spinosissima* is obvious, for it is the prickliest of roses, the stems are covered with sharp thorns and usually with small bristles as well. One of its earliest descriptions is that given by Dodonaeus in his *Herbal* of 1575, where he writes (translation by Henry Lyte), 'Amongst the kindes of wilde Roses, there is founde a sorte whose shutes, twigges and branches are covered all over with thicke small thornie prickles. The flowers be small single and white, and of a good savour. The whole plant is base and low, and the least of al both of the garden and wilde kind of Roses.'

In his *Herbal* of 1597 Gerard calls it the 'Pimpinell Rose' and tells how it acquired this name as well as that of Burnet Rose: 'The Pimpinell Rose is likewise one of the wilde ones whose stalks shoot forth of the ground in many places, the height of one or two cubits, of a brown colour and armed with sharp prickles, which divide themselves towards the tips into divers branches, whereupon grow leaves consisting of divers small ones, set upon a middle rib, like those of Burnet, which is called in Latin *pimpinella,* whereupon it was called *R. pimpinella,* the Burnet Rose.'

This edition of Gerard's *Herbal* has a drawing of the Burnet Rose entitled 'Rosa Pimpinelle folio, the Pimpinelle Rose' and tells of how it 'grows very plentifully in a field called Graies (upon the brinke of the river Thames) unto Horndon on the hill, insomuch that the field is full fraught with them all over. It groweth likewise in a pasture as you go from a village called Knightsbridge unto Fulham, a village thereby, and in many other places.' One can imagine the lovely sight, fields of white roses in flower, and their wonderful scent spreading far and wide.

I have often wondered when the Burnet or Pimpinell Rose began to be called the Scots (or Scotch) Rose, and so I searched for early plant lists. Nurseries and nurserymen date from very early times – the first London nursery was in existence around 1560 – but the first mention of Scotch Roses I found was in a bill dated 1775, for plants supplied to the Countess of Oxford by John and William Perfect of Pontefract: '4 Burnet-leaved Roses 1s 4d; 2 Red Scotch Roses 2s; 2 White Scotch Roses 1s 4d.'

So in the late eighteenth century they were already being called Scotch, while the description 'Burnet-leaved' was also still in use.

Raising the Rose

It was not until 1793 that Robert Brown began to raise his double coloured Scotch Roses and brought out the small list which started the extraordinary rise of the popularity of these roses. And extraordinary it was, beginning with a small list of eight roses! This is the account Robert Brown gave to Joseph Sabine, F.R.S., some twenty years later, on how he raised his roses:

In the year 1793 Robert Brown and his brother transplanted some of the wild roses from the hill of Kinnoul near Perth into their nursery garden. One of these bore flowers slightly tinged with red, from which a plant was raised whose flowers exhibited a monstrosity, appearing as if one or two flowers came from one bud, which was a little tinged with red: these produced seed, from whence some semi- double flowering plants were obtained; and by continuing a selection of seed, and thus raising new plants, they in 1802 and 1803 had eight good double varieties to dispose of: of these they subsequently increased the number, and from the stock in the Perth garden the nurseries both of Scotland and England were first supplied.

The eight double roses were, as far as Sabine could ascertain: 'The small white; the small yellow; the lady's blush; another lady's blush with smooth foot-stalks; the red; the light red; the dark marbled; and the large two-coloured.'

From this small beginning the Scots Roses rapidly became very popular. About fifteen years later those Perth roses were acquired by Robert Austin of Glasgow who cultivated them until he had over one hundred new kinds. By around 1820 there were many collections in nurseries and private gardens throughout the country and in London and its environs. They were at the peak of their popularity from then until about 1840 and an extraordinary number of varieties were listed.

There must have been many roses that were very similar, even identical, for in 1827 Messrs. Dickson of Edinburgh had one hundred in their catalogue and later Austin & McAslan of Glasgow listed 208 varieties. In 1830 *Hortus Brittanicus* gave 177 varieties which, except for thirty, all had names, but, alas, no descriptions. The unnamed thirty, however, gave colours, for example 'double crimson' and 'light marbled'. Otherwise these long lists are incomprehensible, fantastic collections of names chosen from place names such as 'Loch Leven', and from towns, titled people and Greek and Roman mythology. Only four of the names from the 177 varieties listed in *Hortus Britannicus* are still in use today, and these we greet with the same comfortable pleasure that we would have on meeting an old friend in a crowd of strangers, on seeing a 'kent' face. They are 'Fulgens', 'Falkland', 'Loch Leven' and 'Staffa'. It seems incredible that all this came from the little wild rose of Kinnoul Hill!

Colour Classification

Sabine, Secretary of the Royal Society, thought highly of Scots Roses and collected and grew many in his own garden. In 1820 he read a paper on double Scots Roses to the Society, going fully into the confusing question of the two names *spinosissima* and *pimpinellifollia*. He considered the latter to be the correct name for the true wild Scots Rose with very small, round leaflets, smooth flower stalks (pedicels), the white flowers sometimes tinged with red. *R. spinosissima* has larger leaves, the flower stalks small spines, and large white flowers with no tinge of red. Sabine was of the opinion that the two should be considered different varieties and that *pimpinellifolia* should be accepted as the correct botanical name for the species.

He went on to describe the Scots Roses he had growing in his garden, listing them by colour, for he had no patience with the fanciful names of the early lists which 'gave no aid to classification or description, and are therefore very objectionable.' He continues: 'A very important advantage arising from the classification by the colour of the flowers will be, that when any variety is raised and established as worthy of distinction, its place in the arrangement will be assigned with ease.' Within each colour section he gave an exact, botanical description of each rose. Here is his list of the roses in their sections.

Section I	*Double White Scotch Roses*
	1. Small Double White
	2. Large Semi-double White
	3. Large Double White
	4. Whitley's Double White
Section II	*Double Yellow Scotch Roses*
	5. Small Double Yellow
	6. Pale Double Yellow
	7. Large Double Yellow
	8. Globe Double Yellow
Section III	*Double Blush Scotch Roses*
	9. Princess Double Blush
	10. Double Lady's Blush
	11. Anderson's Double Lady's Blush
	12. Dutch Double Blush
	13. Double Provins Blush
	14. Double Pink Blush
	15. Double Rose Blush
Section IV	*Double Red Scotch Roses*
	16. True Double Red
	17. Double Light Red
	18. Double Dark Red
Section V	*Double Marbled Scotch Roses*
	19. Double Light Marbled
	20. Double Crimson Marbled
	21. Double Dark Marbled
Section VI	*Double Two-coloured Scotch Roses*
	22. Small Double Two-coloured
	23. Large Double Two-coloured
Section VII	*Double Dark-coloured Scotch Roses*
	24. Small Double Light Purple
	25. Double Purple
	26. Double Crimson

Popularity and Survival of the Scots Rose

The Scots Roses were welcome, bringing as they did the first foretaste of summer as the spring flowers were fading, and since their sudden emergence into popularity in the early 1880s they have always had their admirers. In *Roses for English Gardens* Gertrude Jekyll writes: 'The Scotch Briers are excellent plants for many kinds of use, but are perhaps best of all in wild banks with Heaths and Cistuses. . .These fine hardy Briers have also one merit that most roses lack, for in winter the leafless crowd of close-growing, plentifully-prickled branches forms masses of warm bronze colouring that have quite a comforting appearance. The pretty Briers might well replace the dull and generally ugly steep slopes of turf that disfigure so many gardens. They are charming accompaniments to steps and their low balustrades; they are equally in place in the humblest garden and the most exalted, and in all sorts and kinds of places and for all kinds of uses they hardly ever come amiss.' She grew them round her house, Munstead Wood.

E.A. Bowles writes of them in *My Garden in Summer* with appreciation: 'I have a great affection for most of them, from the dwarf native form, with its small cream-coloured flowers, to the double garden-raised forms known as Scotch Briers . . . I could almost believe that *Rosa spinosissima* represents the first attempts of the gods in fashioning the rose, for its dwarf, wild form is a centre from which branch off so many different types.'

In *Shrub Roses of Today* Graham Stuart Thomas writes: 'They are nearly as prolific of their flowers as they are of their leaves and thorns. A bush in full flower is a wonderful sight; the wiry shoots bending under the weight of the blossoms, and the whole creating a brilliant effect. Mere plenitude would not be enough, however; they fortunately have a sweet charm of their own, an exhilarating fresh scent – like lily of the valley in its revivifying purity – and they flower in early summer just when we are ready to welcome roses, before the hot days of midsummer bring forth the greater garden varieties.' He also writes, as did Gertrude Jekyll, of their 'maroon-black hips, round and shining like huge black currants. . .Towards autumn these dark fruits often add to the remarkable display of sombre leaf colour, grey-brown and plum colour vie with maroon and dark red in intensity, with an orange or yellow leaf here and there.'

But a decline came with the advancing and constantly increasing tide of new roses with their brilliant colours and long-flowering periods. Both the old shrub roses and the Scots Roses were being gradually swept away, and more was now expected of roses than that they should be like shrubs, once-flowering. The Scots Roses certainly come into flower earlier, before any other roses, and are deliciously scented, but by the beginning of July they are over. And it must be admitted, they are extremely prickly and have exuberant, widely running suckers. But they have great charm, and one has only to see a bush or hedge in the full flush of flowering on a sunny June day, and enjoy the scent which spreads all over the garden, to realise how delightful they are and how much we would miss them.

Nevertheless, the numbers continued to decrease, and fewer and fewer appeared in

nurserymen's catalogues. By 1848 William Paul in *The Rose Garden* listed only seventy-five. He began by saying, feelingly: 'Well has this rose been named "spinosissimus" for it is indeed the most spiny of all roses, and the spines are as sharp as they are plentiful.' But by the time Paul was writing most of the early, very lengthy lists with all their fantastic names had disappeared, and Paul's list gives a whole set of new, unfamiliar names. Those early lists are perhaps only of interest now in showing the popularity of the roses, the variety of names that were invented, and the great number of different seedlings the Scots Rose could produce.

In 1936 Edward Bunyard, in his book *Old Garden Roses,* carefully and lovingly describes thirty-six varieties and hopes that many more may be discovered. By 1965 McFarland gave only fifteen in his book *Modern Roses*, and when Richard Thomson wrote his foreword to the new edition of Paul's book he commented: 'When we consider the Scotch Rose and its first rainbow variations and find that Paul offered 75 of them, the mind boggles. Most cannot be found today.'

However, there were still gardens, such as Gertrude Jekyll's, where old roses were grown and cherished. And although banished from modern gardens, Scots Roses were still to be found in little country gardens, the refuge of so many old-fashioned plants. There they remained, climbing over and through the surrounding dry-stane dykes, covering them with an abundance of sweet-smelling flowers, so that, with winter past and summer come the old folks used to say 'the bonny days are here again'.

I think the double yellow Scots Rose was the most common in the eastern part of Aberdeenshire. I remember it so well all up and down Donside, and even yet one can come on a bush of these yellow roses by a garden gate in a village – there is one I often pass in the village of Old Rayne. In the garden of my early childhood there was a great old bush of yellow Scots Roses, so high that I could only just reach up to the little round flowers with their wonderful scent.

Yet in spite of their neglect, Scots Roses have a great capacity for survival. When I moved to Balbithan in 1960, I found several old bushes in the garden. They had possibly been there since about 1840 when the neglected garden was restored and many roses were planted. There were five different kinds, two pinks, a marbled rose-pink, a semi-double deep rose, and a lovely two-coloured one, which I believed from descriptions to be 'Mary Queen of Scots'. To these I added others – two pinks, a white and a yellow from the old Manse garden of Echt, Aberdeenshire, to make a hedge. More recently I found two more at Craigievar Castle, and from Crathes Castle I brought 'William III'. Others, all different, I have found – one in a garden at Fortrose, another by the roadside near Cuminestown, and a fine hedge of a red rose at Kinloch Rannoch. There must be others still surviving in old gardens, or even beside ruined cottages, such as the rose that was found by the tumbled stones of a long-deserted, lonely Speyside cottage. And here is the story of another rose, Prince Charlie's rose, as told me by Alex Duguid, from the records of Edrom Nurseries in Berwickshire where it grew, and where he worked for many years with the Misses Logan-Home, who founded the nursery. Alex Duguid recounted the story thus:

> After the battle of Prestonpans in 1745, where Charles Stuart defeated the Government troops commanded by Johnnie Cope, on the evening of that day a reception was held in the ballroom of Holyrood Palace at which the prince wore on his coat a double white rose. On the morning after the prince had gone the chambermaid found the rose left on the dressing-table in the bedroom. She took it home to her mother, a keen gardener, who managed to root the rose spray. Eventually the resulting plant was planted in the gardens of Carberry Towers [probably Lady Elphinstone's home] where it flourished. Many years later Mrs. Cowan, eldest sister of Miss Mollie Logan-Home of Edrom, was having tea with Lady Elphinstone who gave her plants of this rose, and Mrs. Cowan in turn gave a plant to her sister who planted it in the garden of Edrom House, Duns, Berwickshire. In 1925, when the Misses Logan-Home moved the Edrom Nurseries to Silverwells, near Coldingham, the rose was planted there and soon developed into a large bush, increasing itself by suckers. Again when I came to Ballater in 1979 I took a plant of this rose with me, where it is spreading and flowering freely. Approximately 3 feet high, it produces many small double white flowers every summer.

I still have a plant of this long-lived rose given me by Alex Duguid.

It should be pointed out that the ''45' took place some fifty years before Robert Brown began raising his double (and coloured) roses, but the doubling of wild flowers is not uncommon, and Scots Roses seed freely, with great variety in the seedlings. Edward Bowles tells how he found striped, pink and deep red forms among the typical white ones 'growing on the Penally Burrows near Tenby'. Gordon Rowley, in his 1961 article 'The Scotch Rose and its Garden Descendants' in the Royal Horticultural Journal writes: 'Wild populations of *R. spinosissima* vary extensively in habit, armature, leaf serration, indumentum and flower colour. Thus, from the head of Loch Coruisk, Skye, Dr. B.E. Godward of London University was kind enough to send me cuttings from an isolated population in which the flower colour varied from yellow to deep pink. Seedlings from wild plants show still greater variation, including degrees of flower doubling, and possibilities as a garden plant were early recognised.'

Rowley then goes on to tell the story of Robert Brown's Perthshire nursery. So the double white Scots Rose that Prince Charlie wore at the Holyrood reception is explained, and we are left to wonder from whose garden it was gathered. As for the other 'Jacobite' roses, *R.* x *alba* 'Maxima' and *R.* x *alba semi-plena*, they have long had these names and their tall bushes were grown at many a cottage door and in many a castle garden of Jacobite followers. These are the roses that were engraved on Jacobite glasses to toast the 'King over the Water'. There are still lively arguments as to which of these two roses is the true 'Jacobite' rose, as there

are, too, over Prince Charlie's rose.

In 1994, Dr. Peter Waister, former Head of Department of the Scottish Horticultural Research Institute, Invergowrie, wrote an account of the Scots Roses in the Royal Caledonian Horticultural Society's Journal. Entitled 'The Scots Briers,' the article described the origin and early development of the Scots Roses.

The following year, Dr. Waister made an expedition to Loch Coruisk to look for the Scots Roses earlier found by Dr. Godward and sent to Dr. Rowley. He found clear pink, marbled and very pale cream varieties among the usual white bushes. Elsewhere there were only white and occasionally a few cream and some pink-flushed-white, or white with just a suggestion of pink.

There are many hybrids among the Burnet Roses, some arisen by chance, their parentage unknown or guessed, others of known origin such as *R. x involuta*, *R. tomentosa* x *R. spinosissima*, which was a spontaneous hybrid first recorded in 1800 from the Hebrides. I have not seen this rose, but Graham Stuart Thomas describes it in *Shrub Roses of Today* as being single, usually white with pink buds and long reddish hips, and as a rapid runner underground. Other hybrids illustrated here include 'Stanwell Perpetual', *R. x reversa*, 'Mrs. Colville' and *R. x hibernica*.

Most of the double yellow roses we see now would appear to be hybrids, crossed with *R. foetida*, the Austrian Briar, which accounts for their deeper colour and less attractive scent. But the true native Scots Rose is paler in colour, smaller, and has the true delicious scent of the species. Three of these double yellow hybrids are illustrated and described here: 'Harison's Yellow' (*R. x harisonii*), raised in 1830, 'Williams' Double Yellow' ('Williamsii') in 1828 and 'Ormiston Roy', produced in Holland by Doorenbos in 1938, and said by him to be 'Allard' x *R. spinosissima*. Wilhelm Kordes raised a series of beautiful hybrids in Germany, of which 'Frühlingsgold', 1937, was the first, but although a Burnet Rose was a parent, they are too different in appearance from the Burnet Roses to be included here. The most recent hybrid, as far as I know, is one raised by David Austin in his nursery, a cross of *R. pimpinellifolia* with his English Rose 'Wife of Bath', with cupped white-centred flowers of soft rose pink. It closely resembles the Scots Roses and so Austin named it 'Robbie Burns'.

I should point out that *R. pimpinellifolia* hybridises very readily with other native roses, such as *R. tomentosa* and *R. canina*. These hybrids are all extremely confusing and best left to botanists. They are fully described by Graham and Primavesi in *Roses of Great Britain and Ireland*, published by the Botanical Society of the British Isles.

Where to See Scots Roses

A place to see lovely roses in all their beauty is at Kinnaird, near Inchture in Perthshire, where there is a splendid collection, one of the most comprehensive in Scotland. When the village school was closed the small playing field was acquired by the District Council and it was decided to make it into a rose garden, concentrating on old-fashioned and Species Roses and particularly the Scots

Roses. The garden was planned and laid out by Dr. and Mrs. Peter Waister and Mrs. Dorothy Park in 1974. The Kinnaird Village Garden is now a delightful rose garden with Scots Roses predominant, and this is most appropriate, for it was here, close to the Hill of Kinnoul in the Carse of Gowrie, that the double Scots Roses were first raised in Robert Brown's nursery. The Scots Roses in the Kinnaird Village Garden include:

'Duke of Argyll'
'Lutea Maxima'
Semi-double white
Double cream
'Loch Lomond'
'Altaica'
'Hispida'
'Dundee'
Hillier's single crimson
'Ormiston Roy'
'Glory of Edzell'
'Harison's Yellow'
'William III'
'Painted Lady'
'Nana'
'Townsendii'
'Andrewsii'
'Lutea'
'Bicolor'
John Innes 'A'
John Innes 'B'
Semi-double from Crathes
'53' single white
One from the Castle of Mey
R. x *reversa*
R. foetida 'Bicolor'

The rising interest in the Burnet Rose reached new heights when Miss Kay Anderson of Bridgend of Lintrathen organised a 'Burnet Rose Day' in 1993 at Alyth, Perthshire, to which came botanists, taxonomists and keen rose growers from all parts of Scotland, all interested in the little Burnet Rose. They brought 158 specimens of flowering branches, which were arranged in colour groups, and forty-five of the most distinctive were then photographed, recorded and numbered to form an archive which can be added to later. Cuttings were also taken for propagation.

Near Pitlochry there is a long roadside bank of the white Burnet Roses, glorious when in full flower, and again near Stonehaven there are stretches growing along the roadsides. I have often thought how pleasant it would be to have these – our native roses – planted along some of the dividing strips of our modern dual carriageways.

Scots Roses Illustrated

One of the earliest illustrations of a Scots or Burnet Rose is that in Gerard's *Herbal*, and since then others have followed. When Mary Lawrance painted roses in 1799 for her book *A Collection of Roses from Nature*, she included five Burnet Roses. Alfred Parsons painted roses for Ellen Willmott's *The Genus Rosa*, and in *A Garden of Roses* five of his paintings of Scots Roses are reproduced along with descriptions by Graham Stuart Thomas. It is interesting to know that Redouté painted seven varying forms of Burnet Rose for his great work *Les Roses*, for which the botanist Claude-Antoine Thory gave the botanical descriptions. It was at first intended that this should be a scientific production, but Thory allowed, among all the talk of 'painstaking research' as to varieties, species and so on, that the roses were also selected for their beauty. And so the book became famous for its beautiful illustrations. I have included the seven Burnet Rose names and descriptive notes as they appear in the Wordsworth edition of *Les Roses*.

Rosa pimpinellifolia mariaeburgensis   'Burnet Rose of Marienbourg'
The first of these roses is the single white Burnet Rose which was found growing in the Alps and in the Ardennes near to Redouté's home country, and was discovered by his brother Henry Redouté. The painting shows a single, rather large, white rose with rounded petals, pink in the bud, which is pointed. It has characteristic round black hips.

Rosa pimpinellifolia pumila   'Dwarf Burnet Rose'
This was said 'to grow on mountains in arid places in Northern Europe. It suckers little and forms layers with difficulty.' The small single white flowers are cup-shaped and are said to remain so almost until the petals fall. The hips are small and black. It is a dwarf shrub with brown stems closely set with prickles. It was said to be 'rather rare in gardens, being neglected on account of its small size, but in spring it offers attractive sprays of bloom. In some German towns it is marketed for its early, sweetly fragrant flowers.'

Rosa pimpinellifolia rubra multiplici   'Double Red Burnet Rose'
This 'rare and beautiful cultivar' is described as 'notable for its elegance and the profusion of blooms in spring'. It grew slowly and produced few suckers, but was readily propagated by grafting. The flowers are a delicate pink and faintly scented. The painting shows only one of the flowers semi-double, and the stamens show prominently in both flowers. The buds are large and rounded, and the stems have many long sharp thorns. Descemet[1] obtained the seed and distributed this rose.

Rosa pimpinellifolia flore albo submultiplici　　　　　'Double White Burnet Rose'
This rose was for long rare and expensive, but in time it was stocked by almost all nurseries under the name 'White Pompon'. Its popularity was thanks to Descemet. In Redouté's painting it appears as a large and beautiful semi-double rose with abundant stamens and large white rounded buds.

Rosa pimpinellifolia major flore variegato　　　　　'Hundred-crowns Burnet Rose'
Descemet had obtained this curiously-named rose as a seedling from a much smaller rose of Du Pont's and Vibert introduced it under the name 'Pimprenelle Belle Laure No. 2'. The flowers are shown as single with rounded petals which shade from deep pink in the centre to pale pink edges and are flecked all over, very like the petals of some of our marbled roses

Rosa myriacantha　　　　　'Thousand-spined Rose'
'Indigenous to the Dauphinè and near Montpellier in dry stony places, it remains unchanged by years of cultivation. It has been considered a variety near *R. spinosissima*, and is indeed related.' [In *Shrub Roses of Today* by Graham Stuart Thomas, it is included under 'the wild Burnet Roses' as *R. spinosissima myriacantha*.] The painting shows a long straight branch with the very long sharp prickles in a close formidable array all along it, and solitary, small, single roses, white tinged with pink at the edges, and their prickly flower-stalks, set at close intervals.

Rosa pimpinellifolia inermis　　　　　'Thornless Burnet Rose'
'Nestler found this wild in the Vosges and sent it to De Candolle. It commonly turns up in sowings of seed of the prickly *pimpinellifolia*, and vice versa'. It is 'unarmed except in extreme youth when minute, ephemeral prickles are to be seen'. The painting shows a branch with several single, white flowers delicately flushed with pink at the edges, long, pink buds, and, of course, smooth thornless stems.

1. Descemet was the nurseryman of St. Denis. In 1815, when the Allies prepared to march into Paris, he had some 10,000 seedlings which were rescued by Vibert and taken to safety on the Marne.

Rosa pimpinellifolia

This is the wild Scots (Scotch) or Burnet Rose. Low growing and very prickly, it spreads vigorously by underground stolons or suckers to form a tangle of small bushes along our coasts. Inland it may also appear on hillsides and river banks. The dark stems are covered with fine bristly hairs and straight sharp prickles. The leaves are small, with seven to nine characteristic tiny rounded leaflets with finely serrated margins. The small, single, five-petalled, white or creamy-white flowers have a delicious fresh scent. The centres have crowded yellow stamens. The flowers are abundant, each singly on a short stalk (pedicel) from the leafy sprigs which are set alternately along the long arching branches. Later they are followed by maroon to black hips, like large blackcurrants, when the leaves take on their autumn colours of brown and plum, with here and there a yellow leaf to add a sparkle.

'Altaica'

This rose comes from the Altai Mountains in Siberia, and was introduced to our gardens before 1820. It is also known as *Rosa pimpinellifolia* 'Grandiflora', and is the largest of the Burnet roses, reaching to a vigorous 5 feet and spreading freely by its suckers, but so lovely in flower that Graham Stuart Thomas writes in *A Garden of Roses* that 'Any resolve to get rid of it entirely, made in winter when one has to dig out its roots wandering far and wide, is broken as soon as its arching branches are again covered with the 3–inch wide, gracious fragrant flowers'. In winter the foliage is purplish and the hips are large and round, turning dark maroon. The leaflets are large, oval and dull bluish-green, while the flowers are creamy with a distinctly lemon tinge, especially in the centre, with numerous stamens. The stems are very prickly, with long pale thorns and bristles.

R. pimpinellifolia 'Altaica' is one of the parents of several hybrid roses; Wilhelm Kordes used it in producing his series of 'Frühlingsgold', 'Frühlingsmorgen' and 'Frühlingsanfang' hybrids in Germany, and it is a parent of the double white 'Karl Förster'.

'Altaica' from Dr. Cusick's garden, Bieldside, Aberdeen

This rose is smaller and deeper in colour than that in the previous illustration. It has numerous small yellow stamens. The flower stalks are smooth, with small red prickles further down the stalk. The young leaves are fresh green, becoming blue-green later; the leaflets are rather small, though occasionally there is a leaf with much larger leaflets, and are sharply notched, sometimes doubly notched. The stems are greenish-brown with long, pale, downward-pointing thorns, mixed with smaller prickles.

(John Innes) 'A'

A single white grown at Kinnaird. This was included in the rose collection of the John Innes Institute when it moved to Norwich in 1967, along with about a dozen other Burnet Roses such as: 'Altaica', 'Andrewsii', 'B' red, Double red, 'Hispida' 'William III', 'Lutea maxima', 'Old Yellow Scotch', 'Painted Lady'.

Double white

A typical double white Scots Rose, with rounded buds and flowers, small rounded leaflets, thorny stems and bristles, and hips that turn black in autumn.

Single white from Bent, Laurencekirk, Kincardineshire

A large strong bush, one of the earliest to flower and always covered with flowers, which are set very closely along the long branching stems. The petals are usually rather twisted or folded, giving the flowers their characteristic appearance, the buds are long, not rounded. The flower stalks and hips have bristles, while the stems have long pale thorns. The mid-green leaflets are oval and often have double notches. The calyx is persistent, and the hips are abundant, very large and intensely black and shiny so that the whole bush glitters. Of unknown origin, and possibly a hybrid.

Double white from North Berwick

This rose, from a cottage garden, dates from before 1926. Unlike most of the Burnet Roses it has a flat flower, not cupped, with small petals curled in the centre; there is no pink in the bud. It reaches to about 4–5 feet, and has an arching habit, and with suckers it becomes a thicket, not a bush. There is a delicious scent, but it is very prickly. This rose resembles 'Nana', one of the Kinnaird roses.

Single cream-white from the Forth Road Bridge

A single, creamy-white, rounded flower, with crowded yellow stamens. The leaflets are grey-green, very round, with large notches. The flower stalks are smooth, and the dark stems have many long, straight, pale thorns, but no bristles. The flower buds are slightly tinted with pink at the tips, and are long, not round.

Double cream-white from Nether Affloch Farmhouse, Dunecht

This is a large old bush, 5–6 feet, with very double flowers, the stamens hidden in the centre of the crowded petals. Both flowers and buds are very rounded, the backs of the outer petals with traces of red. The sepals are short and narrow. The flower stalks are smooth, and the prickles on the stems small. The leaflets are dull, dark green and rounded.

33

'Dunwichensis'

Commonly known as the 'Dunwich Rose', it was found at Dunwich in Suffolk some years ago, but its date and parentage are unknown. The flowers are single cream shading to lemon in the centre, fading to white as it ages, the mass of yellow stamens enhancing its brilliancy. It is prostrate in habit, the long branches lying on the ground studded along their full length with pale cream roses, gradually mounding up into a low rounded bush. The young shoots are red, thickly covered with innumerable sharp thorns, also red, but there are no bristles. The tiny blue-green leaflets are rather oval, their finely notched edges reddish.

Double white from the author's garden, Sunhoney, Murtle,
near Aberdeen

This has a globular bud and flower with smooth pedicels, and dull green, rounded leaflets. The stems have both thorns and bristles. A double white from the Balbithan garden is very similar, as is one from the nursery at Edrom, near Coldingham. It is deliciously scented – a fresh lily-of-the-valley scent.

Semi-double white from Kinnaird

The large flower opens to reveal small petals along with the stamens in the centre. Traces of pink in the opening bud fade when the flower has opened. The large leaves have up to about nine leaflets, larger than usual and long. The stems are green and bristly, with no long thorns. It is probably a hybrid.

Double cream-white from Ardfern, Argyllshire

The buds are completely globular and the flowers still rather round on opening, but very double, almost quartered like a Centifolia Rose, with smaller petals in the centre along with the stamens. There are few thorns and no bristles. The leaves are dull green, rounded and finely notched.

'Duke of Argyll'

The large, single, creamy flowers are tinged with pink, with sometimes a streak of deeper pink on both back and front of the petals. The buds are bright pink. The pointed leaflets are more oval than round and finely notched; deep blue-green they turn darker as they age. The stems are very prickly, the flower stalks bristly, while the short flower stems have small red bristles. The hips are long, oval, red turning dark.

Single cream from the author's garden, near Aberdeen

This resembles 'Duke of Argyll' but has smaller flowers, the petals are cream with delicate veining of pale pink, and are heart-shaped. The long pointed buds are white, flushed pink. The small rounded leaflets are dull green. The stems are very thorny, with red bristles and pale thorns.

Single blush from the author's garden, near Aberdeen, and from Bent, Laurencekirk

The small round flowers, at first cupped, then opening flat with petals curling back, are soft pink becoming white in the centre. The pedicel is smooth. The buds are pointed and bright pink. The leaflets are small, rather pointed, and fresh green when young, becoming darker when older. The brown stems are very prickly with both bristles and short dark thorns.

Single pink and creamy-white from Kinnaird

Single flower with a distinct soft pink band circling the centre, the petals creamy-white at the margins, centres and on the reverse. The sepals are long, narrow, and tapering to a point. The flower stalks are slightly bristly, the leaflets small, rounded and bright green. The red-brown stems have many straight pale prickles. The painting is from a young plant which may grow to 3 or 4 feet.

'Glory of Edzell' from Bent, Laurencekirk, Kincardineshire

A tall erect bush with long arching branches which are set all along with single delicately veined bright rose flowers with conspicuous white centres. The calyx is long and narrow and the flower stalks smooth. The thin, brown, flowering stems have long straight prickles, rather spaced out, and the main stems are strong and densely armed with straight white thorns. The leaflets are very small and dark. This is one of the first to flower. A graceful and beautiful rose.

Single pink from Contlaw Mains, near Aberdeen

An attractive single pink, the colour is deeper at the edges of the petals where it is faintly marbled; the centre is creamy-white. There is an occasional extra petal. The flower stem is smooth, and the red-brown stems have rather sparse long straight thorns. The leaflets are small and fresh green.

Double pale-rose from Cocker's

A fine example from the garden of Ann Cocker, Whitemyres, this is very double with rather narrow, deeply cut petals of a delicate pale rose, the outer ones reflex, giving the flower a somewhat ragged appearance. The pedicels are smooth and the sepals long and narrow.

Single unnamed rose

The petals are delicate rose-pink at the edge shading to white, with similar reverse, and yellow in the centre. The dark stems have long thorns but no bristles.

'Cocker's Blush'

From the garden of Cocker's Rose Nursery, this is a double rose, almost white, with the centre petals faintly blush. The flower stalks are smooth, and the dark red-brown stems are well armed with prickles.

Double lilac-blush from the author's garden, near Aberdeen

The pale petals turn outward at the edges but the flower remains globular, the colour deepening in the centre. The small rounded finely serrated leaflets are a rather dull green and there are small prickles at the back. The red-brown stems have short brown prickles but no bristles and the flower stalks are smooth. This rose is from a large old bush.

Double blush from Bent, Laurencekirk, Kincardineshire,
originally from David Austin

The pale creamy flowers, with a faint blush which deepens in the centre, are creamy-white on the reverse. The calyx is short, tinged with red, and the pedicel is bristly. The leaflets are small, rounded, dull green, and the stems are light brown with both thorns and bristles.

Semi-double from Newton of Stracathro, Angus

A delicate shell-pink, semi-double flower which opens wide displaying the centre of golden stamens. The leaves are fresh green, becoming darker. The flower stalk is bristly, but the stems have few thorns and no bristles.

Double blush-lilac found by David Bromley in Norfolk sand dunes

The delicate colouring opens from a rounded bud to a rounded flower, the stamens barely showing, the petals paler on the reverse. The flower stalk is smooth, the leaflets small and round, the stalks reddish; there are few thorns.

'Falkland'

A delicate blush, reminding one of the lovely Alba Rose 'Celeste'. The flower is rounded, double, with curving petals that have slightly rolled-back edges. Along with 'Lady Hamilton' it is one of the most beautiful of the Burnet Roses. Its dull, leaden green leaves provide a perfect background. The flower stalks are smooth. The dark stems have long straight thorns and there are tiny reddish prickles along the backs of the leaves.

'Stanwell Perpetual'

This is a most delightful and greatly treasured rose, for it is sweetly scented, repeat flowering, and most delicately beautiful. It appeared as a chance seedling in a garden or hedgerow at Stanwell, Essex, and was put on the market by the nurseryman Lee of Hammersmith in 1938. It is presumed to be a cross between *Rosa pimpinellifolia* and an Autumn Damask, from which it inherits its repeat-flowering habit and shape of flower, for it opens from a blush-pink cupped bud to a large, double, cream-flushed-pink flower, with rather quilled petals and a button eye. It grows into a large bush, up to about 5 feet, with prickly stems and grey-green foliage. It is unique among the Scots Roses in that it is repeat flowering.

'*Andrewsii*'

This is one of the few old named Burnet Roses that have come down from the past. It is named after Henry C. Andrews who wrote *Roses…1805–28*. The rounded double or semi-double flowers are of a specially clear true pink, enhanced by the dark leaves. It grows into a dense leafy bush with dark stems that have thorns but no bristles, although the leaves have tiny red prickles at the back. In describing it in *A Garden of Roses,* Graham Stuart Thomas says Miss Willmott recalled it was common in French gardens.

Double pink flush from Mergie, Kincardineshire

The large bush of this creamy-white rose is covered with very rounded buds faintly tinged with a pink flush which deepens in the centre as they reluctantly open into rounded, very double flowers. The calyx is narrow and tapering, the flower stalk is smooth; further down the stem has red bristles, while the main stem is red-brown with both bristles and long pale thorns. The leaves are dull blue-green and rather oval.

Double cream-pink on house wall at Balbithan, Aberdeenshire

A tall, very strong bush which suckers freely. The flowers are double, cream slightly tinged pink, globular in bud, but later opening wide to show the stamens, the petals reversing at the margins. The calyx turns back when the flower fades. The flower stalks have tiny bristles, and the stems have rather short, dark thorns as well as bristles. The leaves are bluish-green, usually more oval than round, with sharp, neat notches, sometimes double-notched.

Semi-double blush from Kinnaird

Semi-double, deeper in centre, the reverse of petals paler. The leaves are rather long. The stems have sparse straight thorns and no bristles. It is late flowering.

'Lady Hamilton'

The cup-shaped, almost white flowers are delicately flushed with lilac-pink towards the centre, and open to reveal the stamens, but still retain their gentle curving shape which shows the creamy back of the petals. The sepals are reddish and taper to a point. The pedicels are smooth. The leaflets are blue-green, finely serrated, more oval than round and usually about nine in number. The young stems have reddish prickles, and the old, dark stems are very thickly set with straight pale thorns.

This was sent to the author by Mrs. P. Taylor, to whom it had been given by a Mrs. Gwdyr-Jones of Erbistock in North Wales. It is said to grow on the hills above Llangollen.

Double blush from the author's garden, near Aberdeen

A large, old bush, high and spreading. The rounded flowers are very delicate creamy-blush, the reverse paler, the petals turning back as they age. The buds are long, the leaflets blue-green and rounded, the flower stalks smooth. The young stems have small pale prickles, dark brown with short pale thorns when old.

Semi-double pink from Cuminestown, Aberdeenshire

A large old bush found at the roadside had cupped buds and semi-double soft pink flowers, the in-curved petals opening to reveal many yellow stamens. The spreading branches had dark brown stems with straight sharp thorns.

Rosa x reversa

A hybrid, *Rosa spinosissima x R. pendulina,* dating from before 1820. This makes a neat bush, suckering freely, with bright green leaves and single, bright carmine flowers with many yellow stamens. The petals are paler on the reverse. The leaflets are very neat, regularly spaced and finely serrated; the leaf stalks and serrated edges are red. The young stems are red, the old ones brown with have bristles. Bowles points out that it gets its name from the downward-pointing, needle-shaped spines on its stems. The hips show its *R. pendulina* parentage – red, oval and nodding.

This rose came from Kinnaird, and was given to Dr. Waister by Dr. Gordon Rowley of Reading University.

Semi-double lilac from Threave, Castle Douglas, Kirkcudbrightshire

A semi-double pale lilac rose with very cupped buds and flowers which show clearly the white undersides of the petals. Later they open wide, displaying the stamens and small curling central petals before fading. The leaflets are small, blue-green and very finely notched. There are thorns but no bristles and the flower stalks are smooth.

'Fulgens'

A small greyish bush, with semi-double bright rosy-pink petals that curve outwards with a paler reverse and which become lilac as they fade. The brown stem is well furnished with straight, light brown, sharp prickles and a few small bristles. The leaves are small, with finely notched, dull green leaflets. Round, dark maroon hips. From Kinnaird.

Semi-double rosy-pink from Dr. Cusick's garden,
Bieldside, Aberdeen

Semi-double rose with globular flowers and buds opening later to show stamens. The rosy-pink petals are much paler, nearly white, on the reverse, which shows up in the opening bud. The sepals are rather broad. The leaves are medium green, pale at the back, small and very finely notched. The flower stalks have tiny bristles, the stems long, fine prickles as well as bristles, and the old branches have long, sharp, pale thorns.

Double deep-pink rose from Kinloch Rannoch, Perthshire

This rose, found forming a garden hedge, was covered with richly coloured double flowers, and made a splendid background to the garden. The bright, deep rose flowers are rounded, opening to show the stamens, the buds are globular, and the calyx lobes rather short. The leaves are dark, blue-green, much paler on the reverse, and the leaflets are round and regularly spaced. The stems are very prickly with small sharp thorns. In shape the hips are flattened and in autumn turn black.

Semi-double pink from the author's garden, near Aberdeen

A rounded bush of about 3–4 feet, with many cupped flowers of soft rosy- pink which tend to be grouped at the ends of the stems and persist in their rounded cup shape for some time. The fresh green leaves are small and finely notched. The stems are very prickly, with long pale thorns mixed with smaller ones. The flower stalk is smooth and rather thick. This rose occurred as a seedling.

Semi-double rosy-purple from Kinnaird

This opens to a rather flat flower, with some smaller, curling petals in the centre. The colour is a soft, rosy-purple, paler on the reverse with a touch of white beside the cluster of yellow stamens, The leaves are fresh green, the leaflets rounded, paler below and sometimes double notched.

'Mrs. Colville'

A hybrid, probably a cross with *Rosa pendulina,* as it has its smooth red-brown wood and long plum-red hips. A large, strong bush, suckering freely, it is covered with rich, deep crimson-purple flowers with vivid white centres – a spectacular sight, one quite startling to come on suddenly. The flowers are single, with occasional odd petals, so that the brilliant white centres are prominent. The sepals are long and reverse as the flower opens. The leaflets are oval, dark green, finely notched, and paler beneath. The stems have sharp thorns but no bristles, although the flower stalks are bristly. From Bent, Laurencekirk,this plant came originally from Kinnordie, near Kirriemuir, near Forfar.

'Mary Queen of Scots'

A lovely and unusual rose, especially in bud and opening flower, when the curving petals reveal the striking contrast between the rich purple-crimson of their inner surfaces and the pale, almost silver, lilac-grey of the reverse. The flower stalks have tiny red bristles and the stems are red-brown, with long straight pale prickles. The leaflets are rounded, with well-marked notches. The sepals are rather short and broad, turning back when fading. It is a beautiful and sweetly scented rose, and tradition has it that it was brought from France by Queen Mary.

(John Innes) 'B'

This is a most interesting and unusual rose from the John Innes Institute, Norwich. It is single with rather small flowers of very deep crimson becoming paler towards the centre. The stamens are its special attraction: these are red and when the flower first opens they are outlined with gold, like delicate filigree; later they become brownish. The leaflets are oval, dark blue-green, paler on the reverse, and set very close together. The leaf stalks and the very fine notched leaflet edges are red. The leaf stalks have small prickles along the back, while the stems have long straight thorns. The pedicels are smooth, the sepals dark.

'*Dundee*'

Double, brilliant cherry-red, opening wide to show stamens, and as the flower opens the edges of the petals turn back to give the flower a pointed, almost ragged appearance. On the reverse, the petals are slightly paler with a yellow base. The sepals are short, dark and reversed, pushed back by the fully opened flower. The flower stalk is smooth. The nine to eleven leaflets are light green on the young shoots and turn a dark leaden green when older; they are rounded and broadly notched. The young stems are reddish with small prickles, but the old branches are very prickly with long white thorns and bristles. This is one of the brightest of the Scots Roses and a bush in flower is outstanding in its brilliancy.

*Single carmine from Dr. McCance's garden,
Strachan, Kincardineshire*

A single, very bright carmine rose with a little white shading to yellow at the base of the petals, which are rounded and notched. The sepals are long and tapering, and the flower stalks smooth. The dark stems are very prickly, with long pale thorns and bristles.

'William III'

This is a dwarf bush, only up to about 2 feet high, which suckers freely, forming a dense, low, prickly thicket. The flowers are fully semi-double, the purplish-crimson petals rather paler on the reverse and turning back as the flower ages, giving it a somewhat pointed look. The flower stalks are smooth and the dark green sepals have white edges which turn back. The small dark green leaflets have purple edges, more pronounced in the young leaves, and paler reverse. Small round maroon hips follow. From Crathes Castle gardens, Kincardineshire

'Balbithan'

This rose, whose origins are unknown, was growing luxuriantly and abundantly in the garden when the author came to Balbithan in 1960. It had obviously been there for many years and, for want of a name, was called the 'Balbithan Rose'. It flowers early, and so was the first of the Burnet Roses seen in the garden. It is a tall, large bush, spreading rapidly with far-reaching suckers, and lovely in flower when the arching branches are laden with abundant, bright rose, semi-double flowers. They are cupped at first, and later open wide to show the creamy centre and the yellow stamens. It is very leafy with large, blue-green leaflets which are much paler on the reverse. The dark stems have bristles and thorns.

'Cherry'

The single flowers are vivid cherry-red, with rather pointed petals which curve inward and are much paler on the reverse. The large yellow stamens have red filaments. The leaflets are small, dull blue-green but a pale light green on the reverse. The young stems are reddish and prickly, with long, straight, pale thorns; the old branches are densely covered with long pale thorns and numerous bristles. The vivid flowers make it a spectacular little bush of about 3 feet high. From the Cruickshank Gardens, Aberdeen University

Rosa x hibernica (R. pimpinellifolia x R. canina)

A rose of Irish origin, having been found in 1795 in County Down not far from Belfast by John Templeton, who sent plants to the National Botanic Garden, Glasneven, Dublin, where it was named 'Hibernica', the 'Irish Rose'. At one time it was plentiful, but owing to road widening and other 'improvements', it became scarce and the last remaining plant was taken to Belfast around 1960, where it still grows. It forms a large spreading bush, and in appearance is much more like *Rosa canina*. The large, single, bright pink flowers are arranged in clusters, the leaflets are larger than those of *R. pimpinellifolia*, broadening towards the tip and sharply serrated. The bristly hips are coloured like those of *R. canina*, but are more rounded. They also have the characteristic long spreading sepals of *R. canina*. There are few thorns. The rose illustrated here came from Peter Beales's nursery and grows in the author's garden.

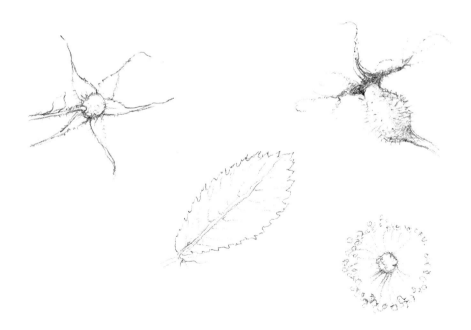

Hillier's single crimson from Kinnaird

The rather long, deep crimson-purple petals are much paler on the reverse. The sepals are long and narrow. The fresh green leaflets are large. The strong young stems are reddish with straight, long prickles. The bush glows with abundant bright flowers.

Single from Kinnaird

This was originally found in an old garden of Dr. Waister's and was thought to be a seedling from Hillier's single crimson (see previous illustrationa). The brightly coloured petals are paler on the reverse.

Semi-double marbled from Balbithan, Aberdeenshire

Deep rose-pink in the centre with little flecks and streaks of deeper pink, the petals are paler, almost white towards the margins and on the reverse. The semi-double flower gradually opens wide displaying the centre with small yellow stamens. The flower stalks are smooth, but the stems are well armed with thorns. The leaflets are small, round and finely notched. This rose was foundin 1960 climbing up an old Irish yew.

Semi-double marbled from Kinnaird

The semi-double pink flowers, with curling, rounded petals, open to reveal stamens and small petals, and are marbled with a deeper shade. The flower stalks are smooth, with reddish prickles on the young wood; the older stems are very thorny with pale curved thorns. The leaves are a fresh green, with small rounded or oval leaflets.

Semi-double marbled with pale margins from Kinnaird

The petals of the rounded flower are bright rose with marbling and paler margins, shading to white in the centre which is filled with many short stamens and curling, smaller petals. The reverse of the petals is pale lilac-white. The leaflets are variable, both rounded and narrow. Slightly bristly. The reddish stems are set with scattered long, sharp prickles.

Semi-double marbled with narrow petals from Kinnaird

This marbled rose has narrower petals and opens more widely than the previous example. The flower stalks are bristly and the stems thorny. The leaflets are dull green and rather oval.

Semi-double marbled from cottage near Migvie, Aberdeenshire

This rose forms a large bush about 5 feet in height. The marbled, semi-double flowers open wide, showing the stamens, and the petals curl outwards with creamy-white margins and centres, so that the deep rose-pink marbling is very distinct. The sepals are long and narrow and turn back. The flower stalks are bristly, and the red-brown stems have reddish prickles. The foliage is dull green, and the leaflets vary from round to rather narrow.

'Hispida'

Like 'Altaica', this rose comes from Siberia. It is one of the earliest to flower. The large, light lemon, single flowers have long buds and smooth flower stalks, and the calyx segments are long and tapering. The leaves are characteristic with long, narrow leaflets, finely serrated, dark blue-green and paler on the reverse and inclined to fold inwards. The stems are red-brown and very prickly with long straight thorns. The hips are large, dark maroon, flattened and smooth. It has been in cultivation since 1781.

Single cream from Kinnaird

The petals are a uniform lemon-cream, rather deeply notched, with very narrow, smooth flower stalks. The oval and rather pointed leaflets, seven to nine in number, are fresh green becoming darker. The stem is very prickly, with many long sharp prickles and bristles.

'Lutea Maxima'

This appears to be a hybrid with *Rosa foetida* as it has the same characteristic scent and vivid colouring – a bright buttercup-yellow. The flowers are single, large, with broad petals and long narrow buds. The leaflets are quite large, oval, bright green and downy beneath. The dark stems have few thorns.

Double cream from Kinnaird

A very double, rounded, deep cream flower shading to lemon in the centre, the reverse paler; the petals curl inwards. The flower stalks are bristly, and the stems have bristles as well as many long sharp prickles. The round leaflets are set very close together, and have well defined wide notches. Originally from the John Innes Institute, where it was named 'Double Scotch Yellow'.

'Ormiston Roy'

The large, single, clear yellow flowers are delicately veined, their colour enhanced by the dark foliage. The leaflets are larger than usual for Burnet Roses and have sharply pointed notches, sometimes doubly notched. The stems have thorns and are bristly when young; the pedicels have tiny bristles. Large, maroon-black hips. This is said to produce flowers again in late summer. Raised by Doorenbos, 1938, and said by him to be 'Allard' x *Rosa spinosissima.*

Double yellow from Old Rayne, Aberdeenshire

This is very typical of the double yellow Scots Roses found in many old gardens in Aberdeenshire, where the large, tall bushes with globular buds and flowers have obviously been for many years. They have stamens as well as smallish green carpels, and small round leaflets. This specimen had long straight thorns and no bristles.

Double yellow Scots Rose

The native yellow Scots Rose in its double form has small, light yellow, globular flowers, slow to open, with smooth pedicels. It has the typical fresh, delicious scent of the Scots Roses. The leaflets are small and round, and the dark stem has many prickles.

Small yellow Scots Roses were among the coloured forms that appeared as seedlings in the wild along with cream, blush, pink, as well as marbled varieties and double forms. A double yellow was among the first eight raised by Robert Brown from the wild Scots Rose he collected from Kinnoul Hill in 1793, and which he referred to as 'the small yellow'. Much later, a yellow form was found by Dr. B.E. Godward among the wild and isolated roses at the head of Loch Coruisk. This native yellow rose is small and paler and has the true sweet scent of Scots Roses, unlike the hybrids which are commonly seen, such as 'Harisonii' and 'Williamsii', crossed with the Austrian Brier, which have a heavier scent.

The rose illustrated here was found growing near Craigievar Castle; a similar one was found beside a ruined cottage at the much written about 'Back of Bennachie'.

'Harison's Yellow' (R. x harisonii)

This rose is said to have been raised by George Harison of New York in 1830. It is almost certainly a hybrid of a Burnet Rose and *Rosa foetida,* the Austrian Brier, the only yellow rose that could then have been used. Before the introduction of the Persian Yellow Rose, *R. foetida* 'Persiana' (a variety of *R. foetida*), the only yellow roses in this country were the little Burnets and *R. hemisphærica,* which was not suited to the British climate.

The rounded double flowers are bright yellow and quite distinct from 'Williams' Double Yellow' in that it has yellow stamens in the centre of the flower, though both roses have the heavy scent of *R. foetida*. The small buds are red. The leaflets are rounded, with a slightly paler reverse. The dark stems have few pale prickles and the flower stalks are slightly bristly. It forms a large, upright, rather gaunt bush up to 6 feet.

'Williams' Double Yellow' (R. pimpinellifolia Williamsii)

This, like 'Harison's Yellow', is a hybrid of the same cross, but is nearer to the Burnet Rose, and has even been mistakenly called the 'Old Double Yellow Scots Rose'. It was raised about 1828 by John Williams of Pitmaston near Worcester (who also raised the Pitmaston Duchess Pear) and came from seed obtained from *Rosa foetida*.

The bright yellow double flowers are distinguished by the green carpels in the centre, and the petals tend to reflex, giving the flower a rather ragged appearance. The buds are globular, the leaflets rounded, paler underneath, the flower-stalks smooth, and the stems have long, sharp, pale thorns and no bristles. It makes a bush about 4 feet high, branching, and suckering freely.

Bibliography

Andrews, Henry C., *Roses…1805-28,* n.d.

Austin, David, *The Heritage of the Rose,* 1988

Beales, Peter, *Classic Roses, 1985*

Bean, W.J., *Trees and Shrubs Hardy in the British Isles,* Vol. IV, 1980

Bowles, E.A., *My Garden in Summer,* 1914

Bunyard, A.E., *Old Garden Roses,* 1936

Dodonaeus, R., *A New Herbal…,* 1575

Edwards, G., *Wild and Old Garden Roses,* 1975

Gerard, John, *The Herball, or General Historie of Plantes,* 1597

Gore, Mrs. C.F., *The Rose Fancier's Manual,* 1838

Graham, G.G., and Primavesi, A.L., *Roses of Great Britain and Ireland,* 1993

Griffiths, Trevor, *The Book of Old Roses,* 1984

Harvey, John, *Early Nurserymen,* 1974

Hillier's Manual of Trees and Shrubs, 1974

Jekyll, G., and Mawley, E., *Roses for English Gardens,* 1902

Keays, E.E., *Old Roses,* 1935

Lawrance, Mary, *A Collection of Roses from Nature,* 1799

MacFarland, J.H., *Modern Roses,* 1965

Paul, William, *The Rose Garden,* 1848

Phillips, Roger. and Rix, Martyn, *The Quest for the Rose,* 1993

Redouté, P.J., *Les Roses* (1817–1824), Wordsworth Editions, 1990

Rowley, G., 'The Scotch Rose and its Garden Descendants', in Royal Horticultural Society Journal, October 1961

Sabine, Joseph, Paper on Double Scotch Roses, Royal Horticultural Society, 1820

Sweet, *Hortus Britannicus,* 1830

Thomas, Graham Stuart, *The Old Shrub Roses, 1955*

Shrub Roses of Today, 1962

A Garden of Roses, with illustrations by Alfred Parsons, 1987

Waister, Peter, 'The Scots Briers', in Royal Caledonian Horticultural Society Journal, 1994

Willmott, Ellen, *The Genus Rosa,* 1910-14

lutea

double white

William III

Hiberneca

Altaica

Single cherry.

"Balbethan"
Rose